MW01225333

Announcing This Winter's
Rattle Chapbook Series Selection...

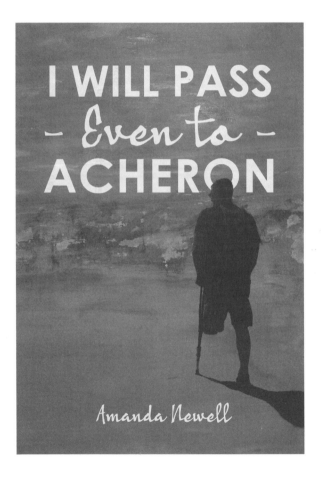

A complimentary copy of *I Will Pass Even to Acheron* by Amanda Newell, the second
of our 2021 Rattle Chapbook Prize winners, is being shipped to each of *Rattle*'s sub-
scribers with this winter's issue. We hope you enjoy! For more information on the
Rattle Chapbook Series, please visit:

www.R a t t l e.com/*chapbooks*

Rattle
12411 Ventura Blvd
Studio City, CA 91604

I WILL PASS
- *Even to* -
ACHERON

Amanda Newell

Rattle | *Studio City, California* | 2021

I Will Pass Even to Acheron
Copyright © 2021 by Amanda Newell

Layout and design by Timothy Green

Cover art by Nancy Mitchell
nancymitchellwriter.com

Adam's silhouette by Amanda Newell

ISBN: 978-1-931307-49-9

First edition

Rattle Foundation
12411 Ventura Blvd
Studio City, CA 91604
www.rattle.com

The Rattle Foundation is an independent 501(c)3 non-profit, whose mission is to promote the practice of poetry, and which is not affiliated with any other organization. All poems are works of the imagination. While the perceptions and insights are based on the author's experience, no reference to any real person is intended or should be inferred.

CONTENTS

ACKNOWLEDGMENTS

Adanna: "Intersection"

Bellevue Literary Review: "Recommendation"

Gargoyle: "Why So Much Grief for Me?"

Pembroke Magazine: "And the Lord God Formed Man of the Dust of the Ground ..." (formerly "First Words") and "Flight"

Pittsburgh Poetry Review: "Adam Drives His Focus"

Scoundrel Time: "For Adam, My Student, in Walter Reed," "Thousands of Spirit Limbs [Were] Haunting as Many Good Soldiers, Every Now and Then Tormenting Them," "Stoic," and "I Will Pass Even to Acheron the River of Pain of My Own Free Will, and with Rapture Even"

The Summerset Review: "Another Adam Speaks"

War, Literature & the Arts: "In Retrospect, He Could Have Come Home" (formerly "438 East") and "On Amputation"

"Intersection" is after Jehanne Dubrow's poem of the same name.

"Recommendation" was selected to be performed by the actor Chris Henry Coffey as part of *Bellevue Literary Review*'s "Off the Page Series" at New York University's Langone Medical Center.

I WILL PASS
- Even to -
ACHERON

For Adam, My Student, in Walter Reed

"Take One!" says the sticky
by the AFG decals,
but I don't, although I want to,
because—really—

I have no claim to sacrifice,
no stump swinging
like a wind-wild bell, no
appled fist, no marbled

skin. Quite possibly
I'm imposing, no better
than a driver slowing
at the scene to count

the bodies, the jellied
patches of blood.
Quite possibly I mean
to stand, unblinking,

in the face of another's,
your exquisite pain.
I am wife, mother, sister,
daughter of no one here.

Whitman rushed towards
the wounded, wrote how
they piled around him
a heap of amputated feet,

legs, arms, hands,
mass casualties and his
longing, grief a hunger,
that must be filled.

These are not like other
hospitals, he wrote.
As with the homeless

woman whose terrible cry
peals in the street, *God, please,*
someone give me something
to eat, I run towards.

I keep my hands open.

~

Recommendation

Dear All, the Headmaster emails,
One of our graduates was seriously

injured by an IED while driving
a military vehicle in Afghanistan.

I push back from my desk.
Adam had been my student

his senior year. *Fractures,*
concussions, other injuries.

Maybe it's not so bad.
But then I think, *We await*

news on his condition means
he could already be dead.

Adam once told me
he'd walked 100 miles

to Ocean City with just
water and a protein bar—

that he'd slept in ditches to be like
those guys who survive for weeks

on an MRE. Although we read
Hemingway and Crane, Adam

wanted to see *the crimson*
clash of war. So I wrote

a letter recommending him
without reservation.

Flight

Somewhere over the Atlantic, a C-130 Hercules
is bringing home racks of soldiers
blown up by roadside bombs or shot in firefights.
Stitched, patched, and anesthetized for the long flight,
the ones who survive won't remember
how their stretchers rattled like teeth with every
dip and pitch, or how their muscles flinched.
In class, a girl asks me if the cute Marine
will be OK, the one who came to visit us
the day before he deployed. I don't tell her he's
packed like cargo in the plane's steel belly,
speeding through the atmosphere at three
hundred miles per hour, the lights of the C-130
pulsing against the sky's black screen.

In Retrospect, He Could Have Come Home

in a flag-draped coffin.
Could have been comatose
or burned beyond recognition.

Sure, they'd do a good job
reconstructing him, but even
the best job could only
approximate who he'd been before

but would never be again,
although traces of the old
Adam would still be there
like a palimpsest: almost,

but not entirely erased.
In retrospect, he'd been lucky.
He came back in one piece,
mostly. Except for his foot,

which refuses to stay
and refuses to go, clinging to him
like a film of dust.
He still looks like himself,

only thinner. In time,
he'll be able to have the dark
chocolate, the driving leg,
the yellow hatchback.

But now, he's dreaming himself
out of time—who knows
where he's gone? Back to 29 Palms
or his M-ATV, or maybe

back to English class.
After we read *No Exit*,
I asked my students
to imagine their own hell,

and in Adam's version,
the clock in his head
is always ticking. No one
can see or hear him.

Intersection

In south Richmond, gang graffiti stains
abandoned buildings, while iron bars fortify
storefronts. Even the homeless vet seems
threatening as he stumbles from car to car
collecting coins while the light's still red.
His rumpled cloak and rusted beard remind me
of Odysseus, who must have looked like this
when he came home disguised as a beggar,
twenty years after sailing off to war.

If I were braver—the kind of person
who isn't afraid of the city's cement terrain,
the ambush lurking in the maze of alleyways—
I would roll down my window and ask
this man if he'd been in the Persian Gulf
or fought insurgents in Afghanistan.
I'd ask him how he drifted here
like a vessel in distress, barely clinging
to the waves. I'd ask that man his name.

"And the Lord God Formed Man of the Dust of the Ground ..."

Adam winces
        when his muscles
spasm, each nerve
        a hair trigger
mechanism for pain
        in his leg,
leg doctors want
        to save, leg
more dust than bone,
        its flesh torn
by sand and shrapnel,
        whose serrated
sharpness he feels
        in his marrow
and craves in his
        throat now
as he strains
        to speak against
the feeding tube,
        his voice gravel,
dry as a desert wind.

Another Adam Speaks

I killed a snake once,
a copperhead.
It must have come
from the river.
We found it
in our yard—
it surprised us
as we were planting
tomatoes and squash.
I took a shovel
and severed its head,
a clean
decapitation.
You have to be
careful with snakes—
their reflexes
are so strong,
sometimes
they'll bite
even after
they're dead.

Still Attached

His foot, cast and wrapped
in gauze, toes sprouting
like sun-scorched weeds—
not even the worst
of what he refuses to call
his combat injuries,
since he was never in
actual combat, unworthy
of the Purple Heart merely
for being in the driver's seat.
So when he wishes himself
dead, I try to imagine Adam
in the underworld, sulking
with Achilles, two players
ejected from the game.
How cruel they can be,
the gods, who know so well
our particular griefs: his
piss-stained underwear
piled in the corner, my shame
at his noticing my noticing,
how we speak of his luck.

Stoic

When I see how swollen and purple it is
and how the skin, like a film of dried glue,
stretches over the bones
of his foot—so clearly now not a foot,
curled as it is like a parenthesis,
already half-afterthought—I wonder if it would be
less painful if it crumbled
onto his white sheets like rain-soaked wood
since it's just one limb
and no longer, he says, any good to him.

On Amputation

Adam, when I look
at the *after* photos

you posted—
how the singed

wires & shredded
metal spill

like entrails
from the M-ATV's

splayed shell,
I can see why

no one thought
you'd survive.

One leg, below
the knee—should I be

relieved that's all
you may lose?

& when you,
practical as you had

always been
as my student,

showed me how
they wired your foot

with pins, it was
only then I noticed

your new right
shoe on the floor.

& your left one,
still in its box.

"Thousands of Spirit Limbs [Were] Haunting as Many Good Soldiers, Every Now and Then Tormenting Them"

Phantom limb pain, the Civil War physician said
when soldiers swore they could feel the *most
inconvenient presence* of their missing
arms and legs, a burning sensation with every
blow ... touch, or ... change of wind.
How many times had Adam posted on Facebook
that he couldn't sleep because his foot was on fire?
Nothing makes sense. Once I watched him
sip dessert from a straw, back when no one
was sure he would make it, when all
he wanted to know was whether the horse-
and-carriage was coming. Those cinder block
rooms at Walter Reed? They're never empty.
For months, Adam refused medication,
insisting he wasn't suffering from PTSD.
He was so proud of his new gun.
Said he slept with it loaded, just like he had
in Afghanistan. *Because,* he said, *you never
know, not even here.*
                    When Silas Weir Mitchell—
that same Civil War physician—treated
Charlotte Perkins Gilman for postpartum
depression, he prescribed rest and *as domestic
a life as far as possible,* to have *but two hours'
intellectual life a day.* A diet *rich in milk and cream.*
I spent so many nights in the rocker
watching *ER* reruns while my son, hungry,
cried in my arms. I could never make enough
milk. But my friends? They pumped bags of it.
My children: little mewling mouths.
So much need. When have I tended to anyone's

other than my own, even now, writing this?
Need, I begin to think, is another word
for selfishness—or, more accurately,
self-destruction. Why else throw my body
on the pyre, if not for the sake of burning?

Third-Grader's Note to Adam Posted on the Wall of Room 438 East, Walter Reed

Dear Adam, I'm sorry
you ran over
a mine. They're well hiden.

Why So Much Grief for Me?

asked Hector after
nine years of war. *No man*
will hurl me down to Death
against my Fate.
So, I ask, if you can't
die unless you're meant to—
until it's time, oh impersonal Fate—
isn't the future now?
I have found 23 signs
on BuzzFeed to prove it:
People are forgetting
to charge THEIR ARMS
(prosthetic). A cashier
dropped my peaches
while I dreamed a snake's
forked tongue spun
cotton candy from sand.
Ground sign awareness:
Keep your camera eye
alert for *disturbance*
to the natural pattern
of the earth. A good *emplacer*
makes the earth lie.
And to think the last thing
I said was, *Don't get yourself*
blown up. I used to say
Don't forget your homework.
Marine Student Handout:
The trick is to look
for precise indicators,
wires, wrappers, boot-
stamped cigarette butts,
other discards, discoloration:
Enemy forces

have been known to
urinate on the top of IED holes.
Take two steps to the left
of those dead, unsuspecting
blades of grass—what do
you get? A black coiling
into blue, hurling you
down into ... fate? A Trojan horse
looks *safe to handle. Benign.*
The man with the face
transplant has made
remarkable progress, yes?
See the photos from after,
and after that. A meds robot
nearly ran me over at the VA.
Steel arms outstretched:
Stay to the right! Stay
to the right! It was so humanly
agitated. None of this
is on BuzzFeed. At the time
of the hospital shooting,
Adam was in his room.
At the time of the shooting.
It was lunchtime, maybe
he was cutting a palm-sized
disc of rubbery meat
with the edge of his fork.
(Nurse Meany was afraid
of what he might do
with his knife.) I like to think
he was blasting Godsmack,
never heard the gun
over the pulse of *breathe, breathe ...*
Maybe he was playing
Lt. Commander Hotshot
on *Black Ops,* where he
gets to be the virtual
first-person shooter. A one-shot-

one-kill sniper.
I think violence
that precise is, always is,
personal. And so,
grief adds to grief,
as when the janitor
shot his friend the Army vet
in the VA parking lot.
One shot. One kill.
Officials called it
an isolated incident, meaning
it was personal,
what Achilles called a curse,
that *brutal, ravenous*
hunger, how it drives a man *down*
the face of the shining earth.

Adam Drives His Focus,

a yellow-orange turbo-charged hatchback with black leather bucket seats,
19-inch rims and a stick shift. Tangerine Scream: a color I'd call ugly

if he hadn't said he liked it because you can't miss him. The wounded warrior
cars—some red Mustangs and Camaros, matte black pickups with tinted
      windows—

are kept in America Garage, where my student unscrews from his left stump
his walking leg, sets it by the front wheel, then screws on his driving leg.

Creeping along the perimeter since he's not ready to go off base, we cruise past
a legless vet in the sun, strapped like so much luggage to a stretcher,

past amputee patrolmen on Segways, past grazing fawns.

.

"I Will Pass Even to Acheron
the River of Pain of My Own Free Will,
and with Rapture Even"

He's signing papers next week—
                    next week   in Coronado—another
              student, gamer kid
who hated school,
                    smoked *Black and Milds*,
                    fought town kids   with glass bottles. He could
already be a Marine—
                    he's got biceps now,
                                        a crew cut, says he's gonna
let loose,   he's gonna kill,
                          he's gonna go
                          to the worst place on earth.   He's gonna
fuck some shit up.

But first he's gonna   run ten miles,
                    put his fins on,   swim from Sandy Point
                          to the moored barge.
                                                  He'll dive
deeper and deeper
                into the dark murk   until he finds it,
                          the anchor,
                          and when he does,
                                he'll tie a red ribbon
                                        around its stem.

Notes

"I will pass even to Acheron the River of Pain of my own free will, and with rapture even" is a line from Nonnos' *Dionysiaca*, 4. 152 ff., Greek epic C5th A.D. Trans. W.H.D Rouse.

The line "These are not like other hospitals" in the poem "For Adam, My Student, in Walter Reed" is taken from the article "The Great Army of the Sick" by Walt Whitman, which appeared in the *New York Times* on February 26, 1863. The line "whole heap of amputated feet, legs, arms, hands" is from the article "Our Wounded and Sick Soldiers," which appeared in the *New York Times* on December 11, 1864. These articles can be viewed online at *The Walt Whitman Archive* <whitmanarchive.org>.

"And the Lord God formed Man of the dust of the ground ..." is from the Bible, Genesis 2:7.

Silas Weir Mitchell, a neurologist and noted Civil War physician, is often credited with coining the term "phantom limb pain." The title of the poem "Thousands of Spirit Limbs [Were] Haunting as Many Good Soldiers, Every Now and Then Tormenting Them" comes from a description Mitchell gave in an 1871 article titled "Phantom Limbs," which first appeared in *Lippincott's Magazine of Popular Literature and Science*, 8 (1871). Mitchell went on to publish *Injuries of Nerves and Their Consequences* in 1872, where he wrote, "Nearly every man who loses a limb carries about with him a constant or inconstant phantom of the missing member, a sensory ghost of that much of himself, and sometimes a most inconvenient presence, faintly felt at times, but ready to be called up to his perception by a blow, a touch, or a change of wind" (348). I have borrowed phrases from this sentence in my poem. Mitchell, who considered himself a poet, was famous for treating Charlotte Perkins Gilman, author of *The Yellow Wallpaper* (1891). Gilman, in a 1913 article titled "Why I Wrote 'The Yellow Wallpaper'?" claimed to have suffered "from severe and continuous nervous breakdown tending to melancholia—and beyond." *The Yellow Wallpaper*, she notes, was a response to the "rest cure" that Mitchell prescribed and to his recommendation that she limit her intellectual activities. Lines from Gilman's letter, reproduced in

Sandra M. Gilbert and Susan Gubar's *Feminist Literary Theory and Criticism* (Norton, 2007), appear in this poem, as does information from the editors' biographical notes on Gilman in their anthology.

In the poem "Why So Much Grief for Me?" the lines "Why so much grief for me" and "No man will hurl me down to Death, against my fate" are spoken by Hector in Homer's *Iliad*, VI. 439ff. Trans. Robert Fagles. The line "… brutal, ravenous hunger drives him down the face of the shining earth" also appears in Homer's *Iliad* XXIV 540ff (Fagles). The *BuzzFeed* article mentioned is called "23 Pictures That Prove We're Living in the Damn Future," by Dave Stopera, December 17, 2016. Lines are also taken from a Marine Warrant Officer Basic Course training pamphlet, "Improvised Explosive Device (IED): W3H0005XQ, Student Handout," USMC, The Basic School, Marine Corps Training Command, Camp Barrett, Virginia. The shooting referenced at the end of this poem occurred on February 22, 2012, at McGuire VA Medical Center in Richmond, Virginia. The victim, James Lee, was shot by Cornelius Hayes, a hospital employee. Details are taken from a February 29, 2012, article in *The Richmond Times-Dispatch* by Reed Williams, titled "Man Arrested After McGuire VA Shooting Confesses."

About the Rattle Chapbook Series

The Rattle Chapbook Series publishes and distributes a chapbook to all of *Rattle*'s print subscribers along with each quarterly issue of the magazine. Most selections are made through the annual Rattle Chapbook Prize competition (deadline: January 15th). For more information, and to order other chapbooks from the series, visit our website.